WALTON WELL

CULTURE ART POETRY FICTION SOCIAL JUSTICE

PRESS

THE WEIGHT OF SOUND

ALSO BY MARIANO ZARO

Decoding Sparrows

Padre Tierra

Tres letras/Three Letters

The House of Mae Rim/La casa de Mae Rim

Poems of Erosion/Poemas de la erosión

Where From/Desde donde

THE WEIGHT OF SOUND

POEMS

Mariano Zaro

WALTON WELL PRESS
Los Angeles   Oxford

Cover art: Leonardo da Vinci, "Star of Bethlehem and other plants"
(between 1505 and 1507), pen and ink over red chalk on paper.
Design & Typesetting: ash good

Theresia de Vroom
Published by Walton Well Press
Los Angeles | Oxford

Paperback ISBN: 978-1-964295-12-1

Library of Congress Control Number: 2025917969

WALTONWELLPRESS.COM

CONTENTS

IV

I

ON A SILVER PLATTER

The world has become heavy, I tell my doctor.
A door handle, a page in a book,
an empty glass.

I want you to see this, she says.
She points at the black-and-white image
on her computer screen.

She wears a wedding band, but I don't want to know
anything about her. I don't want her to have a husband,
children, parents, siblings.

This is your spine, she says. *From C-1 to L-5. Do you see these spots?*
Yes, I say. *What are they?*
Sadness, she says.

Are you sure? I ask.
It's a clear case, she says. *The location,*
the shape, the density.

Same patients present transparent sadness. We call it
Type Zero. Very difficult to diagnose, even using a dye for contrast.
Yours, however, is translucent. Type 1.

And, it's shaped like pellets. You see? Very common in Type 1.
Type 2, the opaque sadness, is shaped like filaments that run
alongside the muscle fibers.

Type 1 stays close to the spine. May cause weakness,
trembling, paresthesia, night sweats,
sexual dysfunction.

There is also Type 3. It's web-shaped, settles around the neck.
Patients describe it as having a bridle around the throat.
Produces speech impediments, sometimes muteness.

The last identified sadness is called Inner Type, she says.
It generates in the amygdala. It looks like a rain
of electrical spores that can reach any part of the body.

Does the Type 1 explain all my symptoms? I ask.
We can't be sure, she says. The research is not
conclusive. But sadness explains many things.

What should I do? I ask.
Some patients try to rest more and calm down.
But sometimes they fall into hypersomnia, she says.

Balance is everything, she adds.
Some patients cry. Some play sports for dopamine
release. Some listen to music. Bach, most of all.

I don't like sports, I say. But I like Bach.
What do you do with your own sadness? I ask.
I just keep plowing, she says.

Will I improve? I ask.
You will, she says. But there is no cure for sadness.
It stays with you, always.

What about the future sadness? I ask.
We will cross that bridge when we get there.
Do you pray, meditate? she asks.

Not really, I say.
How can the body function with all this sadness? I ask.
Nobody knows, she says.

*But some scientists theorize that the body wouldn't
be able to function without sadness.
Just a hypothesis.*

*Do you think we could survive
a lifelong load of sadness delivered in a single day?* I ask.
She plays with her wedding band.

Imagine your sadness, all at once, on a silver platter, I say.
All at once, she says, *on a silver platter,
like the head of John the Baptist.*

EXOSKELETON

metal
leg braces

           that extend
           bend

under the soles
of his feet
inside the boots

           a crutch
           in the left hand

when he sleeps

           the metal braces
           the crutch

also sleep

           they sleep
           on the floor
           next to him

cold
the metal braces

           are cold

when they sleep

           I also sleep
           next to him

his shoulders
his chest
his arms

           are warm

his legs are
not

           never warm
           the legs

he says

> *don't forget*
> *to leave your armor*
> *on the floor*
> *tonight*

he says

> *stay close*

SYNAPSE

In the late 19th century, most scientists believed the brain was composed of a continuous tangle of fibers. Santiago Ramón y Cajal produced the first clear evidence that the brain is composed of individual cells, later termed neurons. The word "synapse" (the space between the end of a nerve cell and another cell) was introduced in 1897 by Charles Sherrington.

Soon, my father says,
you will put two silver coins over my eyes.

*You are going to be out of the hospital
in a couple of days*, I lie.

Neurons are not all directly joined in a reticulum.

The nurse has just left. *The oxygen saturation is low*, she has told me.
My father plays with the bed sheets,
as if kneading the fabric, making a nest.

Why is the ceiling so far away? my father asks.

Information from other cells enters neurons
through dendritic tentacles, and exits
via a gap at the end of long axons.

He lifts his right arm, the one not attached to the IV,
and picks up imaginary fruits.
Perhaps delicate eggs—partridge or quail.
He places them on his chest.

What are you doing, Father? I ask.
I am bringing all this home, he says.
Nobody should be hungry.

        In a neuron, the axon ends.

Is everybody back? my father asks.
Don't forget to lock the door.

Fewer neurons willing to reach across the synapse void.

My father will die with his eyes open.
As if asking a question.

THE MERCY OF MEMORY

Cúbrete la cicatriz.
Cover your scar.

> Her right elbow shattered in a car accident, or
> a ski accident, perhaps the non-accident of war.

There is also a platinum plate,
and two screws.

> She wears long sleeves,
> even in the summer months.
> *Pero no te quejes. But don't complain.*

And, don't say "screws," say "pins." It's softer.

> She doesn't go to the pool,
> to the beach. Doesn't go out much.

The first known use of the word "scar"
was in the 14th century.

> *Tell me again, how do you say "scar" in Spanish?*

As if a scar could have a nationality.

> One night,
> she wears a sleeveless dress.

What happened to you? they ask.
It's nothing, she says. *I don't remember.*
I'm not good with etymologies.

And she covers the scar
with her constant embroidery of silk
and small daily consolations.

AT THE STUDIO

my dance teacher tells
                    me
my dance teacher gives
                    me
a stone

                    heavy
                    dense
                    warm
in my left hand
my dance teacher tells
                    me
to hold

                    smooth
                    bigger than a big fist
                    bigger than a big heart
tells me to dance
                    a stone
the first step
to dance

                    now
                    and one, two, three, four
and I dance

                    lopsided
                    tilted
                    slanted
                    askew
the first step
I dance

                    embarrassment

my dance teacher tells

        me

to dance

        happy embarrassment

        we all carry stones, you know

my dance teacher tells

        me

        just look around

THERMOSTAT

Turn down the thermostat, it's so hot here, my mother says.
She is sitting in a wheelchair near the window.

The thermostat is a white plastic box on the wall.
It has a small digital screen, two buttons the shape
of a triangle—plus and minus, a dial with tiny indentations,
and the on-off switch. It doesn't work.
The nursing home has central heating,
but you cannot control it from the bedrooms.

Are you my son or my grandson? How old are you?
Are you my son, the one that lives far away,
in that faraway country?
Why don't you want to have children? she asks me.

It has been snowing all morning. Just stopped.
Look at the snow, she says, *so clean.*

I am reading a brochure the doctor left earlier.

> Brain cells lose their ability to communicate with one another.
> Two abnormal structures called plaques and tangles
> are prime suspects in damaging and killing nerve cells.

Let's go outside, my mother says.
We cannot go outside, Mother, in this weather. I tell her.
At least open the window. I cannot breathe, she says.

Plaques are deposits of a protein fragment called
beta-amyloid that build up in the spaces between nerve cells.
Tangles are twisted fibers of another protein called tau
that build up inside cells.

Take your children to the park. Play with them, she tells me.
Snow is wasted when you don't have children.
Open the window. I want to feel the cold.

I don't think we can do that, I say. *You may get sick.*

Who cares if I die today or tomorrow? Open the window, she says.
Just for fifteen seconds, I say. *Hope they don't see us.*

Newer research suggests that this type of brain disease
is mainly an autoimmune disorder.

I take the bed's comforter and swaddle my mother,
wheelchair and all, like a cocoon. *Fifteen seconds,* I say.

I open the window. The cool air enters the room,
like a giant, like an ice river. *Fifteen seconds,* I say.
And we count together, whispering, and I close the window.

AFTER THE DIAGNOSIS

The diagnosis was not precise.
It was not a name, an acronym,
a statement. For him, it was a noise.

Time will tell.
            Maybe some of the tests
                        should be repeated. This is
a diagnosis by exclusion.
            A spinal tap, lumbar puncture,
                        has been helpful, not always,
in similar cases.
            But it's painful, you know.
                        And it wouldn't change
the treatment. Perhaps you are
            in the very early stages
                        of something. And you already
have been referred
            to behavioral health services.
                        We have support groups,
counseling. We have checked
            all the boxes, haven't we?

That's when the patient left.
Then, he took a train, and another.

He thought that moving
would push the symptoms away.
That the distance would create
a space, like a valley or a meadow
between the body and its pain.

They have seen him helping the homeless,
cleaning their wounds with gauze and ointment.
They have seen him hitting a dog
with a wooden stick.

They have seen him in museums,
standing in front of paintings,
without blinking, for a long time,
as if beauty could cure anything.

They have seen him kneeling
before altars, burning fires
on an empty beach, at night,
waiting for the worries to dissolve.

He only wants to forget the symptoms,
without trying. Like when you change
trains and you leave behind your lunch box
with a half-eaten sandwich, or a book
you are reading, the ticket tucked between
two pages, or an old umbrella.

But he cannot forget the body
because the body doesn't forget you.

The body follows you wherever you go,
and sleeps with you every night,
like a lover who cannot breathe without
your lungs and, without your eyes
cannot wake up the next morning.

II

MANDARIN AT THE EDGE OF A WHITE FORMICA TABLE

He serves green tea in terracotta cups.
I don't like green tea, but I pretend.

On Wednesdays, after class,
I walk with other students
to the French professor's apartment—
one-bedroom, well lit,
windows facing the university park.

We talk about French cinema.
Film d'auteur, he says.

>François Truffaut, Jean-Luc Godard,
>Jean Renoir, Alain Resnais.

I want to be entangled with all these names
in the dome of his mouth.
His lips are dry, parched.
It's the wind in this city, he says.

I know by heart the marks of his upper front teeth
on his lower lip, like an engraving.

>Roger Vadim, Agnès Varda,
>Jean Cocteau, Éric Rohmer.

I go to the bathroom and open the medicine cabinet
just to see the bottle of vetiver cologne
that I don't dare touch.

Can I help you clean up? I ask.
The other students say goodbye, I stay
and take the teapot and a couple of cups to the kitchen.

Claude Chabrol, René Clair,
Jacques Tati, André Téchiné.

It's a galley kitchen, narrow. On a wall, a big poster
of the movie *Belle de Jour* with Catherine Deneuve.
The lower part of the poster is splashed
with small, oval-shaped stains of tomato sauce.

Claude Lelouch, Bertrand Tavernier,
Louis Malle, Jacqueline Audry.

Let me give you some mandarins, he says.

His fingers expand over the fruit bowl.
He takes eight mandarins, four in each hand.
He presses them against my chest,
and I end up holding them in my arms
as if holding a baby. *Do you need a bag?* He asks.

I wouldn't know what to do with all these, I say.
I may take just one or two.
I lean over the table and drop the mandarins
as softly as I can. I don't want to bruise them.

One mandarin rolls toward the edge
of the white Formica table.
I think we both want the mandarin to fall, but it doesn't.

ANNUNCIATION

We are in the Prado Museum in Madrid
as we have been many times.

You want to see *The Annunciation* by Fra Angelico.
It was restored last year.

We hear a guide talking to a group of visitors.
The Annunciation was painted between 1425 and 1426.

It is composed of four panels, she says.
The canvas itself was in good condition

but the colors were covered by layers of pollution and dirt.
Like the lapis-lazuli in the virgin's robe.

There were also heavy retouches.
Most of all in the angel's right wing.

The guide wears a pink blouse, soft pink,
and a name badge with her photograph.

In the photograph, she looks much younger,
like a different person.

The museum used a silicone gel to clean the surface
and bring back the original light, she explains.

She is right. The colors are fresh, brand new.
I almost miss the old dirt, you say.

I ask, *Do you want to go to the museum store?*
That's the best part of going to museums, you say.

Do you see that man there? You ask.
He looks like my father.

Yes, he does, I say. There is a man
eating a sandwich at the museum café.

He is alone, wears a navy-blue blazer,
silver cufflinks. Shaven head, vivid eyes.

The man coughs a couple of times, drinks water,
looks across the café as if waiting for somebody.

You stop in the middle of a corridor.
We sit for a moment.

My father was so good at hiding things.
And then he did what he did, you say.

Do you think of him often? I ask.
More often now than when he was alive, you say.

A young boy passes by. He carries a coloring book.
He looks at us, smiles.

That boy has perfect teeth, you say.
Some people are born with perfect teeth, I say.

His real name was not Fra Angelico, you say.
What was his real name? I ask.

Guido di Pietro, you say. *When he entered*
the Dominican Order he became Fra Giovanni da Fiesole.

You know everything, I say.
Things that have no use, you say.

Only after his death he became who he is, you say.
Only after his death he became Fra Angelico.

VAPORETTO

It's late and we take the last vaporetto
to go back to the hotel.

We will be there in no time at all, I want to say.
But I don't say anything because
we are not talking much today.

After a couple of minutes, we realize
that we have taken the wrong vaporetto,
in the wrong direction, that we are trapped
where we don't want to be.

You remove your small backpack,
drop it on the floor.
I lean my forehead against a windowpane.
The glass is wet, cold.

>Our sense of touch is controlled
>by a network of nerve endings
>and touch receptors in the skin
>known as the somatosensory system.

There is no place to sit.
We are next to each other, standing, unstable.

>There are mechanoreceptors for movement,
>nociceptors for pain,
>thermoreceptors for temperature,
>proprioceptors for location and position.

I try to caress your neck.
You move away.

I wonder if there are receptors
for the skin to say
how it wants to be touched.
Receptors for repulsion.

CANDID, AS REMEMBERED

Sometimes the Latin teacher
removes her glasses
and talks to us as if we are not there.
We take notes, probably imprecise.

The word *candid* comes from the Latin *candidus*.
It means "white," "shiny."
That's why the white fungus that causes thrush
is called *candida*.

Until the 1950s *candida* was reported to be found
only in the mouth and genitals,
but now it sometimes invades the deeper body,
where it can grow on the heart and other organs
like mold on fruit.

In ancient Rome, candidates were called *candidates*
because they wore white togas.
Children were also dressed in white clothing.
Candidus described the color of the fabric.

The first definition of *candid* in the English dictionary
is not "white" though, it is "truthful," "honest."

I want to believe that the attributes of children—
to be truthful, honest—infused the color of the fabric,
and the word *candidus* expanded its meaning.

Linguists say this is a plain case of semantic broadening.

Children didn't know what they were doing.
Didn't know their souls changed the meaning of words,
the way we speak, the way we understand one another.

READING THE DIARIES OF
PATRICIA HIGHSMITH

On July 26, 1967, Patricia Highsmith writes
"My oldest snail died today."
She says that the snail was born
"around late September 1964"
and "traveled from England to America and back,
went to Paris five or six times, to Majorca and Tunisia."

Snails appear often in Highsmith's writings.
I once read her short story *The Snail Watcher.*
I had forgotten it.
The snail in her diaries
brought back the story to me.

Memory is magnetic. Memories attract one another.

When I was a child, my father told me about snails.
They are hermaphrodites,
but they still need each other, he said.
I had to look up *hermaphrodite* in the dictionary—
a heavy volume, almost too big for my hands.

Why do snails have antennae? I asked my father.
They are not antennae, they are tentacles, he said.
Their eyes are on the tip of each tentacle, you know.

The more you remember, the more you see.

Snails can hibernate for long periods of time.
They produce a white membrane, like silk
or tissue paper. It's called epiphragm.
They seal themselves.

With memory we travel in the spiral of time,
until we realize that the world we remember
does not exist anymore.

My father placed an empty snail shell
in the palm of my hand. It was almost
transparent, so light you could blow it away
like a dry blade of grass.

ENZYMES

They are sitting at a table next to mine
in a small restaurant in Madrid,
near Atocha Station.
Father and daughter, I assume.

> Saliva contains enzymes that help catalyze
> chemical reactions in the body.

She is eight, maybe ten,
wears a summer dress—
white cotton with
small printed lemons.

> The major enzymes in saliva are salivary amylase,
> salivary kallikrein and lingual lipase.

I order a salad, mineral water—
something simple,
I don't like eating alone.
They order veal with mashed potatoes.

> Salivary amylase breaks down starches
> into smaller, simpler sugars.

When she drinks, the girl
lifts her glass with both hands.
The father is young, tells the waiter
to bring a spoon, an extra napkin.

> Salivary kallikrein increases
> vasodilation and capillary permeability.

The girl has short hair,
wears glasses fastened
to the back of her head
with a wide elastic band.

        Lingual lipase breaks down triglycerides
        into fatty acids and glycerides.

The father picks up
a small piece of veal with his fingers,
chews it slightly with his front teeth,
makes a paste
and puts it in his daughter's mouth.

        Another enzyme is acid phosphatase,
        which frees up phosphoryl groups from other molecules.

The girl smiles——gums swollen,
starts chewing, swallows,
looks at her father, grabs the spoon,
clenches her fist——the spoon
rattles against the plate.
She starts eating the mashed potatoes.
The father rests both hands on the table.

        Saliva also contains lysozymes that kill bacteria,
        viruses and other foreign agents in the body.

The restaurant looks brighter now,
even the street traffic is gentler.
I feel less alone.
I may order a glass of wine after all
to celebrate her victory.

TRANSFERENCE

Take the scarf with you, he says.

       In order to extract their scent, petals or whole flowers
       are placed on a large framed plate of glass,
       smeared with a layer of animal fat.

He unties the scarf from his neck,
gives it to me.

       The scent is allowed to diffuse into the fat
       over the course of 1 to 3 days.
       The process is then repeated by replacing
       the spent botanicals with fresh ones
       until the fat has reached a desired degree
       of fragrance saturation.

Thank you, I say.
We are at Heathrow airport.
My plane leaves in twenty minutes.

       This procedure was developed in the 18th century
       for the production of high-grade concentrates.
       It is called enfleurage.

The scarf is the color of wine,
with small polka dots,
slightly frayed,
warm, like a tired dog
sleeping in the sun.

EXPOSURE

The summer
brought you back.

> Not the tentative, early summer.
> The furniture still cold and sleepy.

Not the last days of summer,
melancholic, licking the forehead
of autumn.

> The heart of summer.

The rooftops offered to the sky
like skinned knees.

> The light— flat, unstoppable.

No place to hide.
No other season.

> — *Has it been already fifteen years?*
> — *Exactly fifteen years and three months, since you left.*

DROUGHT

You come at three in the morning
and sit on the foot of my bed.

I know you are not really here.
You are in London,
probably preparing your lunch.

But I see your profile in the mirror,
I feel your weight next to me.

What are you doing here? I ask.
You couldn't sleep, you say,
I wanted to keep you company.

I am a bad sleeper, you know, I say.
Yes, I know, you say,
you have not changed in all these years.

The room is quiet, the window wide open.
On the night table
markers, lip balm,
an old journal, my cell phone,
small bottles of water.

*You always have so many bottles
on the night table,* you say.
It's fear of thirst, I suppose, I say.

The air is crisp. The trees outside
are watching us.

You have shaved your beard, I say.
Yes, you say, *it was itchy*.

The dog sleeps on the floor,
next to the chest of drawers.

This dog, I say, *I bought him a brand-new bed,
but he likes to sleep on the floor.*
You say, *He may have his reasons.
We just don't know.*

Can you hear the ocean? I ask.
Is that the ocean? you say.
*I thought it was the freeway. There are
freeways everywhere in this city.*

I did not shave my beard because it was itchy,
you say. *It made me look older.*

We are getting old, aren't we? I say.

The dog wakes up, walks towards you,
smells your legs. You touch his head,
play with his ears.
Cockers have the best ears, you say.

*Could you stay a little longer? There is a cotton
blanket in the closet if you get cold*, I say.

I will stay until you go back to sleep, you say.
I'm not in a hurry.

Remember the day you prepared the bath
and the steam rose over the bathtub
and formed a perfect cloud? I ask.
I remember, you say. *It was a private cloud,*
just for us. We looked at it like children.
Yes, I say, *as if we had seen a cloud for the first time.*

The dog wants to jump onto the bed,
and you help him. *He has arthritis,* I say.

Will you come in the future,
even if I can't remember who you are? I ask.
I will come back, you say.

You look good all clean shaven, I say.
But you always looked good.

Try to sleep now, you say.
Listen to the ocean,
as if for the first time.

III

THE BIOLOGIST DOESN'T SEE WHAT
SHE WANTS TO SEE

The biologist takes a break.

She leaves the lab for a few minutes,
has coffee, calls a friend
who just had a tough breakup
with an unreliable boyfriend.

You're a strong woman, the biologist says.

The biologist returns the phone
to the chest pocket of her lab coat.
She notices that the pocket has a small hole,
the size of a dime.

She walks back to the lab,
sits on her chair and places a slide
under the microscope.
Soon, a thin thread of sand
starts pouring from the hole in her pocket.

The sand keeps falling,
forms an island around her,
covers the entire floor of the lab.

At the microscope she doesn't see
what she wants to see.
She places another slide,
adjusts the ocular lenses.

The sand covers the hallways,
rolls downstairs and buries
everything that
she doesn't need at that moment—
old microscopes
piled up in dark utility rooms,
the main lobby,
her car in the parking lot,
the lower quad,
university dorms,
the library,
all her years in college,
the semester abroad, in Germany,
high school dances,
her then boyfriend, who had a subtle stutter,
the unsuccessful piano lessons,
her parents' divorce
when she was in second grade,
everything except that day,
at age five,
on the farm where she grew up,
that day when, for the first time,
she saw a calf being born,
and how the mother cow
could not stop licking her calf,
over and over again;
the half-shut eyelids,
the glistening head.

SOME NOTES ON HOW TO GROW STRAWBERRIES

He doesn't know what do to, where to go.
Listen to your inner voice, people tell him.
Find a hobby— painting, gardening.

He tries gardening.

>Take one strawberry, scrape at the seeds,
>place them on a paper towel to dry them out.

He keeps seeds in small envelopes
with handwritten labels.

>Find seedling pots (as many as needed).
>Fill up each pot with soil, pour a little water.

Sometimes he mislabels the envelopes.
Seeds look alike, they are so small,
so insignificant, they weigh almost nothing.

>Get your seeds,
>and let one or two fall into the middle of each pot.

Each seed knows the road ahead,
and the road behind.

>Your seeds will germinate and create
>small visible seedlings in around 2 to 3 weeks.

The seeds know what to do.
Even the ones in the wrong envelopes,
even the ones with no labels.

PORTRAITS

It is as if I knew them,
the people he painted.

        Henry Lamb was born in Adelaide, Australia, in 1883.

In a painting,
a boy reads a book—
indolent purple tie,
muted pocket square.

        Lamb's family moved back to England in 1885.
        In 1907 he studied at the Académie de la Palette in Paris.

Another painting.
Another book, a girl reading—
blue hair ribbon, simple,
blue jacket, blue sweater.
Then a woman, his second wife,
also reading—
red armchair, red book cover.
And another girl,
looking almost straight forward,
book open on her lap—
gray wool skirt, heavy.

        Lamb married Nina Forrest in 1906.
        The relationship was short.
        In 1938 he married Pansy Pakenham.

The portraits have enough
precision, enough casualness.
And everybody is young—
they have long fingers,
luminous faces,
a certain abandonment,
they have time.
Time to finish the page
they are reading,
time to leave the book,
still open, upside down,
on a table nearby,
and come back later.

He was a Trustee of the National Portrait Gallery
from 1942, and of the Tate Gallery from 1944.
Henry Lamb died in 1960
at the Spire Nursing Home in Salisbury.

The books are all closed now,
I suppose. Forgotten.
Perhaps tumbled in garage sales,
flea markets, secondhand stores.
Perhaps in basements
flooded by summer storms
or long winter rains.

MEN AS THEY UNDRESS

Some men undress and cover their chests—
arms folded like the front legs of a praying mantis.

The waistband of their underwear is flaccid but the socks
are tight and print deep grooves on their shins and ankles.
They tilt their hips backward.

Some men undress and tilt their hips forward.
They also walk around with their arms slightly open,
as if their armpits were irritated, had a rash.

They like mirrors, towels, soap, body lotion, talcum powder.
When having sex, they become enthusiastic, acrobatic.

Some men undress, drop their arms and grab
their genitals, softly, one hand on top of the other.
They look down sometimes, like war prisoners.
Sometimes they look up, neck stretched, jaw clenched,
the Adam's apple protruding, angular, defiant.

Some men undress and when they remove their shirt
and leave it on a chair, for example,
the shirt becomes a fountain, then a lake.
They cannot see the lake or the fountain, just the shirt.

You can swim in the lake if you want, or cup your hands
and wash your face, drink if you are thirsty.

Sometimes they walk in the rain, alone, without hurry.
Talking with them for a while you cannot tell
if they are naked or fully clothed.
Dogs lick their hands.

When they die, earth takes them in like lost children;
and you understand that they are going back home.

They don't leave much behind—a few coins, a pocketknife,
a white handkerchief with no initials—clean, neatly folded.

ORCHIDS AND OTHER ANIMALS

I sleep here now, he says.
The house has become too big.
I don't dare enter the bedroom.

He is in the middle of the greenhouse—
an old shed extending through the garden
with tall iron frames and glass panels.

There are ferns hanging from the ceiling,
some empty pots on the floor, long tables,
orchids everywhere.
Each orchid with a cardboard label.
On each label, in pencil, a name,
a number, sometimes a symbol, a date.

Would you like some coffee? he asks.
He cleans a mug with the watering hose,
pours the coffee from an electric coffee maker.
There is no milk, he says.

How long have you been sleeping here? I ask.
Since the funeral, he says. *It's going to be a year*
next month, you know.

From the greenhouse you can see
the empty pool, the main house
with slanted tiled roofs,
the kitchen windows.

Your TV is on, I tell him.
It's always on, he says,
so it looks like somebody is home.

He is much thinner than the last time I saw him.
I want to tell him, but I don't.

What happened to the orchids
that smelled like chocolate? I ask.
The Oncidium Sharry Baby, he says.
I had hundreds of them.
They all died last winter.
Could not save them.

I brought you this, I say.
I give him a set of watercolor brushes,
the thinnest brushes I could find.
He uses them for pollination.

Thank you, he says.
He leaves the brushes on top of a table
with other tools—toothpicks,
tweezers, Q-tips.

Next to the table, a lamp, blankets,
the couch where he sleeps.
Do you want me to stay tonight? I ask.
He pretends he doesn't hear me.

I grow these orchids now, he says.
Habenaria Radiata, the White Egret Orchid.
They look like birds, you see.

Birds in mid-flight, I say.
But they don't go anywhere, he says.

We hug before I leave.
His shoulder blades are sharp.
He combs my eyebrows with his thumbs,
as he used to do.
Pollination, he says.

MEDICATION REPORT

May I have a straw? he asks.
My hands are shaking.

I get a straw from the counter
at the 18th Street Café.

He looks small, hunched, his iced tea
spilling on the table.

It's the new medication, he says.
I get it once a month now.

I thought it was once a day, I say.
That was methadone, he says.

He still has long hair, tight
in a ponytail.

I walked to that methadone clinic
every single day for years, he says.
Now they have me on Sublocade.

What's Sublocade? I ask.

It's like Suboxone, he says.
But it's not a pill, it's an injection.
They poke you in your belly.

Is this better for you? I ask.

It's more convenient, he says, *once a month.*
But I still have cravings.
Thoughts, fleeting thoughts.
This is yet one more thing they try
to calm you down.
They have to kill you a little, you know.

He wears a black T-shirt
and a flannel shirt, unbuttoned.
The shirt is too big,
loose in the shoulders.

Do you still play guitar? I ask.
Not with these hands, he says, *I can't.*

We met when you were in the School of Music, I say.

At UCLA, he says. *I played classical guitar then.*
And you also had a rock band, I say.

Always between things, he says, *never landing.*
Didn't know where my heart was.

Would you care for something to eat? I ask.
Don't have much of an appetite, he says.
Maybe we could share a bagel.

That sounds good, I say.

Sometimes the past feels so empty, he says.
Sometimes, so crowded.

What kind of bagel do you want? I ask.
It doesn't matter, he says. *But no poppy seeds.*

Do you think your hands will improve? I ask.
The shaking, I mean.

I don't know, he says,
but I would love to play again,
something to soothe this mind,
even if just for a minute.

AN ELEMENTARY SCHOOL IN LOS ANGELES: AFTER THE SUMMER BREAK

There is no air conditioning and I ask the principal for a fan.
The custodian brings a fan to the classroom,
but the fan is old, more like a turbine, industrial,
loud, so loud I cannot hear the students when they read.
I have to turn it off.

We are all sweaty and sticky and I tell the students
we are going to clean the desks today, yes, with soap and water.
Go to the sink, open the faucet, wash your face, get a paper towel,
or two, clean your desk, or not, splash all you want, who cares.

I go to Ernesto's desk, I lean over,
and before I say anything, he tells me
I know I can't wash my face here, maestro, I know.
Ernesto's left eye is covered with an adhesive patch
the color of caramel. He is ten years old.

Ernesto went to visit his grandmother in the summer and playing,
playing with other children, playing with canes and reeds
by the river, something happened, algo me hirió el ojo maestro,
this is what he tells me, something wounded my eye,
it was nobody's fault.

And then he says hospital, infection, antibiotics,
speaking more like an adult than a child, he says septic infection
and surgery and second surgery, scarring, eye socket,
molds and casts, temporary prosthesis and revisions.
And now I have to wait for the permanent one, he says,
I have to wait. The doctors are all very nice to me, very nice,
and I still can do everything, maestro, it doesn't hurt.

Today I want to say what you told me in that classroom,
Ernesto, so many years ago. That it doesn't hurt.
I want to say it with your conviction, without blame.

FIRST COMMUNION

I go to her classroom at lunchtime.
We both work in the same elementary school.
Her lights are off today. I knock at the door.
Mrs. Medina, Second Grade. The sign reads.

She opens the door. *Come in,* she says.
We sit in the students' chairs, as we always do.
I brought fruit for lunch, grapes.
Would you like some? I ask.

I am not hungry, she says. Her lunchbox is unopen.
This is my present for Amaranta, I say.
Your daughter must be very excited,
her first communion is Sunday.

Yes, Sunday, she says. *Everything is happening so fast.*
Mass is at noon. I hope you can make it.
I say, *I will be there.* She says, *Thank you for the present.*
You shouldn't have bothered.

I leave the small box on her desk.
I didn't know what to buy so I ended up getting
a small pendant—a silver four-leaf clover,
for good luck.

I met Amaranta when she was a baby. She was named
after the character in *One Hundred Years of Solitude.*
I got the test results yesterday, she says. *Cannot be worse.*
Are you sure? Did you get a second opinion? I ask.

This was the second opinion, she says.
There are so many advances now, so many treatments, I say.
There is no treatment, really, she says. *Just palliative.*
My mother also died young. She removes her glasses.

Do you mind helping me with this? She asks.
I don't want to stay after school, I have no energy.
She passes me her students' artwork,
and I put it on a bulletin board with clear pushpins.

Put this one up there, she says.
I told my students to draw their favorite season.
I say, *What do they know about seasons, these kids?*
There are no seasons in Los Angeles.

That's true, she says. *It's always spring here.*
Or that's what we want to believe.
Put this one in the center, please.
This one with the double rainbow.

SMALL TALK

I'm ready for small talk at this birthday party.
The restaurant, near Malibu,
has large windows facing the ocean.

I'm a peripheral guest,
sitting at a table with other peripheral guests.
The woman next to me wears a floral blouse,
with puffy short sleeves.

The waiters bring the appetizers.

I am ready for

      -Oh, you have an accent, are you Italian? She may ask.
      -No, I am from Spain. I would answer.
      -Oh, Spain. I was in Barcelona once… She may continue.

But that's not the way the conversation goes.
She tells me that she has spread her parents' ashes
the day before.
Here, in the Pacific? I ask.

It was a murder suicide, she says.
The ashes, yes in the Pacific.
You can rent a boat for that, it's a business now.
Do you know what a murder suicide is?
I found them. They were in the car,
parked in the back of the house.
They had been married for over fifty years.
But my father was sick. Emphysema,
breathing problems, you know.
And my mother was recently diagnosed.

A tumor, multiple ones.
My mother did not answer the phone.
This is before I went to the house, I mean.
And my mother always answers the phone.
They were in the front seats of the car.
My mother on the driver's seat.
Which is strange because my mother
hadn't driven for years.
They were fully dressed, boots and all.
As if they were going somewhere.
My mother even had her winter scarf.
The car windows were up but I could see
inside. My father still had the gun
in his hand. The brain, pieces of brain
on the windows, most of all my mother's,
that side of the car, that window.
And not as much blood as one would expect.

What's the first thing you did, I ask,
when you found them?
I had the phone in my hand, she says,
but I couldn't call the police.
It took me a while.
They had it all very well planned, my parents.
But I didn't know.
We don't know
what's going on in people's heads, do we?
They left a note on the kitchen table,
and the driver's licenses, together, touching,
one next to the other,
like twins, both expired.

IV

INHERITANCE

Swallows, swifts—
over the rooftops—
scream, fly in circles.

I'm with my sister
in my mother's house.
What's left of my mother's house.

I brought the power of attorney, I say.

The birds announce the storm.
The sky is a sudden night,
at noon.

Do you think anyone will buy
this old house? My sister asks.
I don't know, I say. *But that's what*
Mother wanted: Wait until I'm gone,
then sell the house, split the money.

Outside, the wind slaps the tree branches.
Let's close the windows, my sister says.

I am leaving tomorrow, I tell her.
Back to California, she says.

There is some furniture left—
a few chairs, an empty bookcase.
In the bedroom,
pill bottles with sun-bleached labels.

I want to keep Mother's winter coat.
The one with the silver trim, my sister says.
Is it here? I ask.

The coat hangs in the middle of the closet,
alone.
My sister checks the pockets—
moth balls, a cough drop.

She folds the coat over her left arm.
We wait in front of a window.
You look like her, I say.

The wind stops, the sky clears.
The birds are quiet.
The rain does not come
today.

We are next, you know, my sister says.
We won't be spared.

THE DISCOVERY OF RED

A single drop of blood, static,
on the tip of my index finger.

> Our blood is red because of
> the heme groups in hemoglobin.

I am wearing my kindergarten uniform—
gray, with white buttons.
My mother did not take me to school today.

I am sick. Low fever.
And it's raining. A ruthless rain—
horse hooves on the roof, pebbles,
small bullets against the windowpanes.

> Hemoglobin is made up
> of four protein chains.

I am playing—I am a mechanic
fixing toy trucks with a plastic screwdriver,
and a needle stolen from my mother's sewing kit.
Boys don't play with needles, she has told me
many times.

This is the first time I see my own blood.
I have seen the blood of animals before,
when killed: chickens, rabbits, pigs.
This is my own blood, my own pain.

> Each protein chain binds to an additional
> ring-shaped chemical structure called heme.

The pain ends all pretense;
I am not a mechanic.
I end where my body ends.
I cry because of the blood
and the loud rain.

        At heme's center sits an iron molecule.
        The iron makes heme look red-brown.

Come here, my mother says. *It's nothing.*
I walk with my finger outstretched,
like a candle, or a lighthouse.

        The iron in hemoglobin binds oxygen
        in the lungs as we inhale.

Don't cry. Don't worry. Your soul
will not leave you. My mother says.
This makes me cry even more.
The fear of my soul leaving my body
through the tip of my finger.

        When the oxygen is released,
        it is replaced by carbon dioxide.

My mother sucks my finger—
her cheekbones sharpen.
She keeps my finger in her mouth.

When carbon dioxide binds to hemoglobin,
the color changes from bright red to dark red
with a hint of purple.

The finger is wet now, cleaned, healed.
That's it, she says.

The protein hemocyanin transports
oxygen in octopuses and horseshoe crabs.

My finger throbs.
Why is my heart in my finger? I ask.
Your heart is in your chest, my mother says.
It doesn't jump around like a squirrel.

Hemocyanin is actually blue.
That's why octopuses and horseshoe crabs
have blue blood.

My mother stops the bleeding.
I stop crying. But she cannot
stop the horses, still
galloping on the roof.

MY SISTER HOLDS MY HAND IN THE DARK

It's not really a theater,
it's bar where young people gather—
they put a projector on the counter,
in front of the tap,
they turn the lights off.

It's 1976, I am twelve,
my sister's twenty-two.
Franco has just died.
She takes me to see
foreign films on Fridays.

Her boyfriend buys me soda, popcorn.
He smokes, everybody smokes.
He has long hair, wears a braided
leather bracelet—silver and turquoise beads.

This is one of those European movies,
my sister tells me. *Not a word to Mother,*
do you understand?

This is the beginning of secrets.

"European" sounds dark, disturbing.
And you know that someone naked
may pop up on the screen at any time.

Not sure if you should bring your brother
to these movies, the boyfriend says.

I am here for the popcorn, I say.

You know he is not like the other kids,
my sister says.

This is the beginning of labeling.

My sister holds my hand
in some scenes:
       shards of glass in *Cries and Whispers,*
       the rape in *Two Women,*
       when Charlotte Rampling dances
       in *The Night Porter.*

I want to be like them, I tell my sister
when we leave.
To be like who? She asks.
Like the people in the movies.

This is the beginning of pretending.

BROTHER

Who is this boy? I ask my mother.
I am pointing
to a black-and-white picture
framed on a bookshelf.
He is your brother, she says.

The toddler is standing
next to a stroller,
wears a small hat.
It's a summer day.

This is not the first time
I have seen the picture.
This is the first time
we talk about it.
I am six years old.

Where is he now? I ask.
He is dead, my mother says.

What happens when you die? I ask.
Where do you go?

Nobody knows, she says.
Everything is the same.
Everything is not the same.

How did he die? I ask.
Fever, dehydration, she says.
What is dehydration? I ask.
He died of thirst, she says.

He was born April twenty-seventh,
nineteen sixty.
He died July eighteenth,
nineteen sixty-one.
It was a Tuesday.

I was born April fifteenth, I say.
Yes, April fifteenth nineteen sixty-three.
It was a Monday, she says.

All my children came to me.
All of them but you,
my mother says. *I looked for you.*
I had to look for you.
Because I was old, they said.

Where was I? I ask.
You were inside your father, she says.

Did my brother have toys? I ask.
Yes, she says. *But I told your aunts*
to take everything away.
His toys, his shoes,
all of his clothing.
You shared the same crib, though.
But not the clothing.
I couldn't do that to you.

Was he better than I was, Mother? I ask.

She touches my hair.
He was strong, she says.
He brought you here.

MOUTH TO MOUTH

> KING CLAUDIUS: Now, Hamlet, where's Polonius?
> HAMLET: At supper.
> KING CLAUDIUS: At supper! Where?
> HAMLET: Not where he eats, but where he is eaten: a certain
> convocation of politic worms are e'en at him.
> (Hamlet. Act 4, Scene 3)

We bury our dog in the back yard.
My father and I. Next to the wooden fence.

The dog weighs 32 pounds, maybe 30 now.
He lost some weight since he was sick.

When we dig in the ground
we hit the roots of the neighbor's cherry tree.

> Roots explore the soil, seeking out
> water and mineral nutrients.

The shovel makes a hard noise
like metal against metal.

It's cold on this quiet October morning.
I wrap the body with a white towel.

I make sure the towel has no stains,
and fully covers his mouth and eyes.

> Once mineral nutrients are dissolved in soil water,
> they move into root cells by osmosis.

We mark the grave with a cross made
of small stones—three horizonal, four vertical.

A crow lands next to the grave,
starts pecking the freshly turned soil.

I wonder if the grave
is deep enough.

> Osmosis is the movement of water molecules
> to a solution of lower concentration.

The rain will scatter the cross stones.
It rains a lot in winter.

Come summer, the neighbor
will bring us his first cherries.

> Osmosis is possible because of the
> cells' partially permeable membrane.

We will eat the cherries—
the sweet and tart flesh.

I keep each pit in my mouth
until it's totally smooth.

Every fruit has its own soul,
my father says.

I will be somebody's food one day—
we become the ones who have eaten us.

VOCATIVE

In the second declension in Latin
masculine nouns change in the vocative form.

The ending -us of the nominative
changes to -e in the vocative.

That's why the poet Catullus,
when talking to himself
in his poem number 8,
does not say "Catullus" but "Catulle":
"Miser Catulle, desinas ineptire"
(Wretched Catullus, stop being a fool).

Nouns ending in -ius change to -i.

When Catullus writes to Iuventius
in his poem number 48,
he does not say "Iuventius" but "Iuventi."
"Mellitos oculos tuos, Iuventi,
siquis me sinat usque basiare,
usque ad milia basiem trecenta,
nec umquam uidear satur futurus"
(Iuventius, If I could kiss
your honeyed eyes, I would kiss them
three hundred thousand times
and never be sated).

Vocative case is used
to address somebody directly.

My mother wakes up screaming
in the middle of the night.
She sits on her bed
and repeats her own name
as if trying to escape a trap.
Neck tense, face flushed,
she repeats her name
until she is exhausted, out of breath.
It's a dream, Mother, I say.
One of your bad dreams.

Her dementia makes her believe
that she is leaving the room.
Call her, she says. *Call her.*
She has to come back.

And I call her. I call you, Mother,
and I cover your shoulders
with your bathrobe.

I call you by your name intact
as it was in your baptism
ninety-four years ago.
I call you by your name dressed
in white for your first communion.

I call you by your name blushing
the day you met Father at age fourteen.
I call you by your name stained
with ashes when you lost your child.

I call you by your name ever-changing
in all declensions: nominative, vocative,
accusative, genitive, dative, and ablative.

I call you by your name and all the names.
I call you by no name at all,
and kiss the top of your head
that smells like sweat.

NOTES

References to books, articles and websites consulted during the writing process of these poems:

SYNAPSE
Rapport, Richard. *Nerve Endings: The Discovery of the Synapse*. W. W. Norton, 2005. This is a book about the scientific achievements of Santiago Ramón y Cajal (1852-1934).

THE MERCY OF MEMORY
Information about the use of the word "scar" is taken from the National Library of Medicine. Full quote: "The origin of the word 'scar' can be traced to the Greek word "eskhara" (in French "escharre"). The word 'scar' was first used in English in the 14th century."

THERMOSTAT
Alzheimer's Association: *What is Alzheimer's Disease?*

ANNUNCIATION
Museo del Prado: *The restoration of "The Annunciation" by Fra Angelico*

VAPORETTO
Resource Center. Homescience Tools: *Sense of Touch*

CANDID, AS REMEMBERED
Online Etymology Dictionary: candid

Bryson, Bill. *The Body: A Guide for Occupants*. Anchor, 2021.
Full quote: "Candida albicans, the fungus behind thrush, until the 1950s was found only in the mouth and genitals, but now it sometimes invades the deeper body, where it can grow on the heart and other organs, like mold on fruit." (Page 36)

READING THE DIARIES OF PATRICIA HIGHSMITH
Highsmith, Patricia. *Patricia Highsmith: Her Diaries and Notebooks: 1941-1995*. National Geographic Books, 2021.
"My oldest snail died today, or maybe yesterday, as Camus would say. Born around late September 1964, died July 25, 1967. She traveled from England to America and back, went to Paris five or six times, to Majorca and Tunisia. She produced some 500 eggs, though she herself was from a deformed batch of eggs, the soil having been too wet. Saved six of batch of eighty. Her shell was also deformed, crusty, like a diseased fingernail. The oldest snail I ever had." (Page 803. Entry of July 26, 1967)

ENZYMES
Thought. Co: *Salivary Amylase and Other Enzymes in Saliva* by Regina Bailey (2019)

TRANSFERENCE
Britannica: enfleurage

SOME NOTES ON HOW TO GROW STRAWBERRIES
Information about how to grow strawberries is taken from this site:
Instructables: *No Budget Strawberries* by Isadwdwadw

PORTRAITS
Information about painter Henry Lamb appears on the right column of the poem and it's taken from Wikipedia.
Wikipedia: Henry Lamb

THE DISCOVERY OF RED
Noë, Alva: *Why Do Many Think Human Blood Is Sometimes Blue?*
NPR Cosmos & Culture, 2017

ANATOMY AND COLOR PENCILS
Brandywine Conservancy: *Butterflies vs. Moths: What Are the Differences?*
Britannica: insect

MOUTH TO MOUTH
Royal Horticultural Society: *How plants absorb nutrients*

VOCATIVE
Catullus. *The Poems of Catullus.* Oxford Paperbacks, 2008.
Latin for Students: *Vocative Case*

ACKNOWLEDGMENTS

My gratitude to the editors of the following publications in which these poems first appeared, sometimes with small variations:

Anacapa Review, Vol. I, Number 6: "Mandarin at the Edge of a White Formica Table"

Beat Not Beat, Anthology of California Poets, Moon Tide Press: "At the Studio"

Interlitq. California Poets: "First Communion," "Orchids and Other Animals," "On a Silver Platter"

Paterson Literary Review, Issue 50: "Brother"

Poetry Goes to the Movies: "My Sister Holds My Hand in the Dark"

Pratik, Special Los Angeles Issue: "Diagnosis of Men as They Undress," "Synapse," "Thermostat"

River's Voice, Río Hondo Community College: "Vaporetto"

Spillway, Issue 30: "Transference"

This book wouldn't have been possible without the guidance and help of my poetry group: Marjorie Becker, Jeanette Clough, Dina Hardy, Paul Lieber, Jim Natal, Sarah Maclay, Holaday Mason, Jan Wesley and Brenda Yates.

Finally, thank you Theresia de Vroom and Gail Wronsky for your encouragement and editing wisdom.

ABOUT THE AUTHOR

Mariano Zaro is the author of six previous books of poetry, most recently *Decoding Sparrows* (What Books Press, Los Angeles, CA) and *Padre Tierra* (Olifante, Zaragoza, Spain). His work has been featured in the anthologies *Monster Verse* (Penguin Random House), *Poetry Goes to the Movies* (Beyond Baroque Books), *The Coiled Serpent* (Tía Chucha Press, CA) and in several magazines in Spain, Mexico and the United States. His translations include *Buda en llamas* by Tony Barnstone and *Cómo escribir una cancion de amor* by Sholeh Wolpé. He is a professor of Spanish at Río Hondo Community College (Whittier, California). www.marianozaro.com

www.ingramcontent.com/pod-product-compliance
Lightning Source LLC
Chambersburg PA
CBHW020758130626
46554CB00006B/2254